David Garfinkel

ADVERTISING HEADLINES *that* MAKE YOU RICH

CREATE WINNING ADS, WEB PAGES, SALES LETTERS AND MORE!

NEW YORK

LONDON • NASHVILLE • MELBOURNE • VANCOUVER

ADVERTISING HEADLINES THAT MAKE YOU RICH

Published in New York, New York, by Morgan James Publishing. Morgan James is a trademark of Morgan James, LLC. www.MorganJamesPublishing.com

The Morgan James Speakers Group can bring authors to your live event. For more information or to book an event visit The Morgan James Speakers Group at www.TheMorganJamesSpeakersGroup.com.

ISBN 9781683501459 paperback
ISBN 9781600370229 eBook
ISBN 9781933596259 Hardcover
Library of Congress Control Number: 2018936706

Cover & Interior Design by:
Christopher & Heather Kirk
www.GFSstudio.com

LEGAL INFORMATION AND DISCLAIMER:

In an effort to support local communities, raise awareness and funds, Morgan James Publishing donates a percentage of all book sales for the life of each book to Habitat for Humanity Peninsula and Greater Williamsburg.

Get involved today! Visit www.MorganJamesBuilds.com

READERS ARE RAVING

"LEADING COPYWRITER TERRIFIED BY THIS BOOK!"

"Alert to fellow copywriters: Big trouble. David Garfinkel has just written a book revealing the secrets behind some of the winningest, money-makingest headlines ever created. Worse still, he tells (and shows!) how any businessperson can modify these winning headlines for their own ads, mailing pieces and internet promotions. What will they need us for?"

David Deutsch, Author, *Think Inside The Box*

"ANOTHER LEADING COPYWRITER WELCOMES BOOK WITH OPEN ARMS!"

"There's a widespread myth that creative people come up with their great ideas out of thin air. But as a copywriter, I'll eagerly seize any tool that helps me write more effective advertising. I've seen a lot of formulas, tips and checklists, but nothing compares with David Garfinkel's *Advertising Headlines That Make You Rich*. It's truly unique, and the concept behind it is ingenious. One of the basic principles of marketing is 'Learn what works — and repeat the successful.' Armed with this clever book, you'll do exactly that. For anyone with something to sell, it's a gold mine of profit-generating ideas."

Don Hauptman, Copywriter/Consultant, New York

"8 NEW HEADLINES... IN NO TIME FLAT"

"Just got done zipping through your book on headlines. **Came up with 8 that I might use for a new booklet I am writing**. Also came up with a good one for an insurance product I am marketing. I wasn't even trying for that one. All this in a half hour."

Frank Meyers, Street Smart Recovery

"SUCCESSFUL ENTREPRENUER FINDS BOOK SUPER-VALUABLE"

"**Next to my computer, I find this book the most beneficial thing on my desk these days. I keep it open** next to my computer because I find I use the concepts to tickle ideas several times each day. It saves me hours of laboring over coming up with ideas from scratch. Now, I just take the ideas from this book and give them my own twist."

Roxanne Emmerich, CEO, The Emmerich Group, Inc.

"THIS IS GREAT STUFF!"

"If you advertise your business in any way, shape, or form, you've got to get this book! In *Advertising Headlines That Make You Rich*, David Garfinkel gives you an abundance of proven, money-making headlines. Each one comes with a short, down-and-dirty explanation about <u>why</u> it works. Then you get a template to show <u>you</u> how to write a killer headline, customized for your business... by only changing a word or two! This is great stuff! I'm buying copies for all my clients."

Bob Brown, Mailing List Resources

"A REAL GOLD MINE"

"You can now write headlines in your sleep with this massive, jaw-dropping, definitive collection of proven headlines. The real gold mine here are the dozens of examples of how YOU can adapt a tested headline to your own needs. This fantastic book could have been called 'Headlines for Dummies.' Anyone can make more money with it. Priceless!"

Dr. Joe Vitale, Author, bestselling *The Attractor Factor*

"SHOULD BE MANDATORY READING FOR BUSINESS OWNERS"

"David Garfinkel has done it again! This masterful writer, in this on-the-button book, provides you not only with 297 killer headlines, but helps you earn $297,000 in extra profits and save $297,000 because now you won't have to run ads with less than superb headlines. If there ever was a book that should be mandatory reading for business owners, this is it. I want to give David a high-five for writing it, but I'll give him a high 297 instead."

Jay Conrad Levinson, Author, *Guerrilla Marketing* series of books

"EASY WAY TO WRITE MILLION-DOLLAR HEADLINES"

"This is the first book on headlines I have ever read that offers an easy way to write million-dollar headlines like a mater copywriter. If you want to know why some people's headlines almost always make money on the Internet, I suggest you read this book. If you don't, you'll hate yourself later."

Ted Kikoler, Internationally renowned graphic designer and copywriter

V

TABLE OF CONTENTS

PART II   THE MAGICAL POWER OF HEADLINES

NOTE FROM THE AUTHOR

THE NAKED TRUTH ABOUT THE FIRST FEW WORDS

H eadlines? Why would anyone write a book just about headlines?

Because, in a print ad, 75 percent of the buying decisions are made *at the headline alone.*

If you are scholarly or scientific (or just plain skeptical), you might ask if I am making that statement solely from my own experience or from rigorous, scientific tests. Here's your answer: While I know it is true from my own experience, I'm quoting in the paragraph above from legendary John Caples. He made that statement in his book *Tested Advertising Methods*.

And Caples, in case you didn't know, was Madison Avenue's acknowledged dean of tracked, measured advertising effectiveness. He had reams of carefully compiled and verified research — based on actual advertising tests — to back up his statement.

Many people spend hours, or days, coming up with a headline for their marketing. Even then, sometimes the headline doesn't work. Why? Because it usually takes years of experience — which includes the painful failures, as well as the gratifying successes — to be able to recognize a headline that has a strong probability of working.

This book does something that many top copywriters privately (and often secretly) do to reduce the risk and in many cases, insure the success, of an ad or letter. It takes <u>proven</u> headlines — which have <u>already</u> been shown to work in the marketplace — and <u>adapts</u> them to other specific businesses. No other book has 297 custom, ready-to-use headlines created from proven winners.

In each chapter there are many examples of headlines that will work for ads, Web pages, letters, email and postcards for a variety of

■   retail businesses

■   business-to-business companies

■   professional service businesses

■   "free agent" (home office/small office) businesses

…and others. There's also a concise explanation of the <u>psychology</u> behind the headlines, which you need to understand to use the headline to get the greatest results for your business. Finally, there's a fill-in-the-blank template that explains exactly how you can adapt this headline to <u>other</u> businesses.

When I told a friend I was writing this book, he asked me a very reasonable question:

"Suppose everyone starts using these headlines. Won't they lose their effectiveness?"

My first instinct was to say, "I don't think that's too much of a problem. Look at it this way. Suppose everyone started saying 'Hi' or 'Hello' when they saw someone they know. Well, they do, you know. And those words are just as effective a way to start a conversation today as they ever were."

But, I realized my friend's question deserved a more direct answer. So here it is:

*Everyone __already__ uses these headlines. Why?
Because they __work__.*

Now, who do I mean by "everyone?" Surely not all advertisers. Many of them have only perfected the art of losing huge sums of money — not the art of writing killer headlines.

No, by "everyone" I mean "all the people who make their livings off headlines that work." Besides direct response marketers — who successfully adapt proven headlines and make fortunes by doing so — these people are cover headline writers for newsstand magazines. They use the same formulas for their work as those you'll discover in this book.

Here are a few random examples of magazine cover headlines from a recent trip to the newsstand:

MAGAZINE HEADLINE & MAGAZINE	PROVEN HEADLINE FROM THIS BOOK
How to Get Air Travel Moving Again ~Newsweek	"How to Win Friends and Influence People"
10 Things You're Not Supposed to Do! ~MacAddict	"10 Ways to Beat the High Cost of Living"
Secrets to a Sexy Body ~Marie Claire	"The Secret of Making People Like You"
7 Signs You're Failing as a Manager ~Sales & Marketing Management	"Do You Recognize These 7 Early Warning Signs of High Blood Pressure?"
Give Us 5 Minutes and We'll Give You A Bikini Body ~Shape	"Give Me Five Days – And I'll Give You The Secret of Learning Any Subject!"

Newsstand magazines depend on impulse purchases from consumers to stay profitable. The headline writers <u>must</u> create enough interest and desire to prompt passers-by to pick up a magazine and buy it — or the magazine goes out of business.

That's why they use these proven formulas. (Notice that they don't use the exact original headline — nor should you — but they use a <u>variation</u>. That's what you want to do, too.)

In fact, the more mass-market a publication is, the more often you'll find the old standards in headlines on the cover. So, as you can see, the headlines haven't "worn out" — they work as well now as they did when they were first written.

Why do they work? I don't know, but I have a theory: The proven headlines work because the original headline writer "lifted" words and phrases from the running chatter in our subconscious minds. The words and structures in these headlines resonate with people at a deep, deep level. It's almost as if they recognize these words as their own thoughts when they read them on paper or a computer monitor — and thus feel compelled to keep reading.

So, when see a headline that would work well if it were adapted for your business, but you don't see the precise variation in the list in that chapter, take a moment to study the other variations. Then read the comments below.

You may be surprised to discover how quickly the right variation somehow "pops" right into your head. Or, if you need to, brainstorm a little, and then you will have <u>exactly</u> the headline you need.

There are many entrepreneurs and marketing managers who deserve much better results from their advertising than they're getting now. Are you one of

■ ■ ■

them? Then this book will be an important first step towards far greater response from your advertising, and overall profitability to your business.

Best Wishes and Much Success,

David Garfinkel

David Garfinkel
Host, Copywriters Podcast
www.CopywritersPodcast.com

PART
I

297 Killer Headlines: *Proven Headlines With Ready-To-Use Variations For Specific Businesses*

CHAPTER 1

Proven Headline: "Get Rid of Your Money Problems Once and for All"

VARIATIONS FOR SPECIFIC BUSINESSES	
Financial Planners	Get Rid of Your Retirement Worries Once and for All
Dentists	Get Rid of That Toothache Once and for All
Headhunters	Get Rid of That Lousy Job Once and for All
Health Clubs	Get Rid of That Sluggish Feeling Once and for All
Caterers	Get Rid of Party Planning Woes Once and for All
Web Designers	Get Rid of Your Web Site Problems Once and for All
Beauty Salons	Get Rid of That Ugly Haircut Once and for All
Stop-Smoking Program	Get Rid of That Nasty Habit Once and for All
Razor Manufacturer	Get Rid of "Sloppy Shaves" Once and for All
Dry Cleaner	Get Rid of That Rumpled Look Once and for All

MORE VARIATIONS FOR SPECIFIC BUSINESSES	
Computer Instructor	Get Rid of "Computer Phobia" Once and for All
Time Management Expert	Get Rid of that Feeling of Overwhelm Once and for All
Health Food Store	Get Rid of Foods That Are Bad for You Once and for All
Security System Installer	Get Rid of Those Sleepless Nights Once and for All

HINTS ABOUT USING THIS HEADLINE

It's so effective because it forces readers to become acutely aware of a problem they have in the area you've identified. For example, anyone who has a toothache is probably somewhat aware of it. But the dentist headline (the second variation, **Get Rid of That Toothache Once and for All**) focuses a reader's awareness of the toothache, and intensifies the pain. This will make the reader <u>much</u> more likely to pick up the phone and call the dentist who is mentioned in the copy of the ad, letter, email or Web page following the headline.

Some important information about all headlines: Headlines that work will either draw your reader's attention to a <u>pain</u> they have or are likely to face, or a <u>desire</u> they have that is not fulfilled.

Either way — whether your readers are in pain or have an unfulfilled desire — this is a problem for them. Your headline gets the readers to expect that you will be able to solve their problem for them.

When you write copy after the headline, to get maximum advantage out of this (or any other) headline:

a) talk about the pain (or desire) you've just identify in the headline, and tell why it will only get worse if the reader doesn't do something about it

b) prove why you can provide the solution to the problem — relief from pain, or fulfillment of the desire — if the reader will take the step of contacting you, and

c) directly invite the reader to contact you, and tell exactly how to do that.

HOW TO ADAPT THIS HEADLINE TO YOUR BUSINESS — "GET RID OF (PROBLEM) ONCE AND FOR ALL"

The key is to make sure you describe the problem using the same words your reader already uses. Let's say, for example, that you are a doctor and you've come up with a Nobel Prize level cure for indigestion. Here's what you wouldn't say in a headline: "Get Rid of Dyspepsia Once and For All."

Why wouldn't you? Because "dyspepsia" is the word you (as a doctor) use for indigestion, but most people reading your ad don't commonly use that word — even if they happen to know what it means. So when they are reading the headline, a word like "dyspepsia" won't register instantaneously with them.

And that's bad. The reason is because what you want to have happen with your headlines if for your entire message to register instantaneously with your readers.

5

To make that happen, you'd use the word or words that are part of their language. What words are those? Probably "stomach ache." So you would use this headline: "Get Rid of Stomach Aches Once and For All."

See the difference? If you're using technical language (like "dyspepsia") in your headline, then you're only "talking" to yourself. That means you're only <u>selling</u> to yourself — and you can only pass that single dollar bill from your right hand to your left hand and back again so many times, before you realize you're not making any money at all.

To make money with headlines, make sure you speak the language of your <u>customers</u>.

HEADLINE BRAINSTORMING PAGE

(Yes, it's okay to write in this book!)

HEADLINE BRAINSTORMING PAGE

(Yes, it's okay to write in this book!)

CHAPTER 2

PROVEN HEADLINE: "WHO ELSE WANTS TO
LOOK LIKE A MOVIE STAR?"

VARIATIONS FOR SPECIFIC BUSINESSES	
Real Estate Agent	Who Else Wants to Live in a Dream Home?
Accountant	Who Else Wants to Pay Lower Taxes?
Discount Carpet Store	Who Else Wants A Beautiful New Carpet — at 50% Off?
Chiropractor	Who Else Wants to Feel Healthy Again — Without Taking Drugs?
Bed and Breakfast	Who Else Wants a Carefree Country Weekend?
Professional Organizer	Who Else Wants to Find Everything at a Moment's Notice?
Web Hosting Company	Who Else Wants Great Web Hosting and Quick Customer Service?
Restaurant	Who Else Wants Home Cooked Food With No Muss and No Fuss?

MORE VARIATIONS FOR SPECIFIC BUSINESSES	
Babysitting Service	Who Else Wants to Go Out Again? (Just Like You Did When You Were Dating)
Copier Sales	Who Else Wants Clean, Crisp Copies at Half the Cost?
Headhunter	Who Else Wants a Great New Job?
Housepainter	Who Else Wants a Freshly Painted House?
Payroll Service	Who Else Wants Their Payroll Handled for Them?
Tire Store	Who Else Wants Great-Looking New Tires?
Wedding Planner	Who Else Wants More Fun and Less Stress at Their Wedding?

HINTS ABOUT USING THIS HEADLINE

This headline taps into the power of "social proof" and "consensus" in a very powerful and subtle way. With the opening words "Who Else Wants...," the headline presupposes that many people already want whatever follows.

Because most people tend to feel more confident about their desires when they know other people have the same desires, this headline puts them in a more receptive frame of mind to read this ad.

■ ■ ■

HOW TO ADAPT THIS HEADLINE TO YOUR BUSINESS — "WHO ELSE WANTS _____?"

How to adapt this headline to your business: Who Else Wants _____? The key is to know what people want as it relates to what you provide, and put it in words that, again, are familiar to them. Be sure to avoid the trap of components and process. Stick to describing the end results you provide your customers.

Here's what I mean: Let's say you sell grass seed. Don't have a headline that says, **"Who Else Wants Better Grass Seed?"** (Grass seed is a component.) You see, no one really cares about the grass seed except the birds who will eat it, and lawn experts like yourself. And don't write a headline like this: **"Who Else Wants a More Rapidly-Growing Strain of Grass?"** (How fast the grass grows is about a process.) People aren't going to watch the grass grow with a stopwatch in their hand. Maybe your botanists do that for a living, but your customers don't.

What should you say in your headline? **"Who Else Wants a More Beautiful Lawn?"** (That headline focuses on the end result you offer your customers.) That's why people buy your grass seed — to have a more beautiful lawn. So feature that in your headline!

HEADLINE BRAINSTORMING PAGE

(Yes, it's okay to write in this book!)

CHAPTER 3

PROVEN HEADLINE: "THOUSANDS NOW PLAY WHO NEVER THOUGHT THEY COULD"

VARIATIONS FOR SPECIFIC BUSINESSES	
Cosmetic Dentist	Thousands Now Smile Confidently Who Never Thought They Could
Camera Store	Thousands Now Take Beautiful Pictures Who Never Thought They Could
Stop-Smoking Program	Thousands Now Have Quit Smoking Who Never Thought They Could
Martial Arts School	Thousands Now Kick-Box Who Never Thought They Could
Denture Adhesive	Thousands Now Eat Corn-On-The-Cob Who Never Thought They Could
Flying Instructor	Thousands Now Fly Planes Who Never Thought They Could
Persian Rug Store	Thousands Now Have Persian Rugs Who Never Thought They Could

MORE VARIATIONS FOR SPECIFIC BUSINESSES	
Lawn Mowing and Hedge Trimming Service	Thousands Now Have Beautiful Lawns Who Never Thought They Could
Luxury Car Dealer	Thousands Now Drive Awesome Cars Who Never Thought They Could
Personal Trainer	Thousands Now Take Pride in Their Bodies Who Never Thought They Could

HINTS ABOUT USING THIS HEADLINE

This works great when you (and others in your field) have helped a lot of people do something they thought they couldn't do — play the piano, for example. People read the headline and think, "Hey — if others can do it, then so can I." And they'll want to read the copy that follows the headline.

HOW TO ADAPT THIS HEADLINE TO YOUR BUSINESS — "THOUSANDS NOW (RESULT YOU PROVIDE THAT MANY PEOPLE THINK IS HARD OR IMPOSSIBLE TO ACHIEVE) WHO NEVER THOUGHT THEY COULD"

HEADLINE BRAINSTORMING PAGE

(Yes, it's okay to write in this book!)

_____

_____

_____

_____

_____

_____

_____

_____

_____

_____

_____

_____

_____

_____

HEADLINE BRAINSTORMING PAGE

(Yes, it's okay to write in this book!)

CHAPTER 4

PROVEN HEADLINE: "BUILD A BODY <u>YOU</u> CAN BE PROUD OF"

VARIATIONS FOR SPECIFIC BUSINESSES	
Personal Coach	Create The Life <u>You</u> Can Be Proud Of
Kitchen Remodeler	Build a Kitchen <u>You</u> Can Be Proud Of
Web Designer	Build a Web Site <u>You</u> Can Be Proud Of
College Admissions Courses	Get Into a College <u>You</u> Can Be Proud Of
Luxury Auto Dealer	Own a Car <u>You</u> Can Be Proud Of
Landscaping Service	Have a Yard <u>You</u> Can Be Proud Of
Office Furniture Store	Have an Office <u>You</u> Can Be Proud Of
Bicycle Store	Ride a Mountain Bike <u>You</u> Can Be Proud Of
Cosmetic Dentist	Have a Smile <u>You</u> Can Be Proud Of
Sculptor	Own Original Art <u>You</u> Can Be Proud Of

MORE VARIATIONS FOR SPECIFIC BUSINESSES	
Architect	Live in a Home <u>You</u> Can Be Proud Of
Personal Trainer	Sculpt a Body <u>You</u> Can Be Proud Of
Jewelry Store	Wear a Watch <u>You</u> Can Be Proud Of
Camera Store	Take Pictures <u>You</u> Can Be Proud Of
Caterer	Throw a Party <u>You</u> Can Be Proud Of

HINTS ABOUT USING THIS HEADLINE

Most people are secretly dissatisfied with some aspect of who they are, what they have or the way they do things. This headline offers them a way out of that dissatisfaction, by promising they can be proud of the same thing they are currently dissatisfied with, or even ashamed of. All they have to do, as you will tell them in your copy, is come to you for help.

HOW TO ADAPT THIS HEADLINE TO YOUR BUSINESS — "HAVE A _____ YOU CAN BE PROUD OF."

To figure out what goes in the blank, as yourself: What is it that changes for the better in the eyes of your customers after they have done business with you? Personal coaches changes lives, Web designers change Web sites, and auto dealers change cars. What does your business change for your customers that they can be proud of? Boil it down to a word or two, and plug that word or those words into this headline.

18

HEADLINE BRAINSTORMING PAGE

(Yes, it's okay to write in this book!)

HEADLINE BRAINSTORMING PAGE

(Yes, it's okay to write in this book!)

CHAPTER 5

PROVEN HEADLINE: "GIVE ME FIVE DAYS — AND I'LL
GIVE YOU THE SECRET OF LEARNING ANY SUBJECT!"

VARIATIONS FOR SPECIFIC BUSINESSES	
Plumber	Give Me 45 Minutes — And I'll Have Your Drain Running Like New!
Internet Service Provider	Give Me 15 Minutes — And I'll Have You Up and Running On the World Wide Web!
Luggage Store	Give Me Half an Hour — and I'll Have You Outfitted for Any Trip You Ever Take!
Personal Trainer	Give Me Half an Hour — And I'll Show You How to Get In the Best Shape of Your Life!
Florist	Give Me Five Minutes — And I'll Send The Perfect Flower Arrangement to Anyone, Anywhere in the World!
Video Production Company	Give Me 10 Minutes — And I'll Tell You How You Can Remember Every Enjoyable Detail of Your Wedding Forever!

MORE VARIATIONS FOR SPECIFIC BUSINESSES	
Speed Reading Instructor	Give Me Eight Hours – And I'll Double Your Reading Speed!
Health Food Store	Give Me 10 Minutes – And I'll Have You Eating Healthy Again
Beauty Salon	Give Me One Hour – And I'll Give You a Brand New Look!
Hair Replacement Specialist	Give Me Three Minutes a Day – And I'll Give You A Full Head of Hair!
Men's Clothing Store	Give Me An Hour – And I'll Give You A Brand New Wardrobe!
Advertising Specialties	Give Me Five Minutes – And I'll Show You How to Keep Your Customers Thinking About You All The Time

HINTS ABOUT USING THIS HEADLINE

It all hinges on <u>a result you provide surprisingly quickly</u>. But before you use this headline, make sure you can really provide that result! Study the personal trainer headline very carefully.

Notice it doesn't promise to get you in shape in one hour. It just promises that the trainer will show you how in one hour. Big difference!

■ ■ ■

HOW TO ADAPT THIS HEADLINE TO YOUR BUSINESS — "GIVE ME (SURPRISINGLY SHORT PERIOD OF TIME) — AND I'LL (GIVE YOU THIS RESULT YOU WOULDN'T HAVE EXPECTED!) "

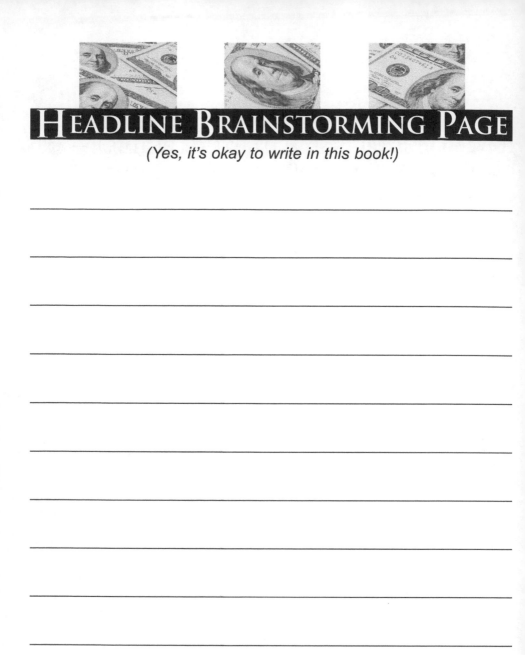

HEADLINE BRAINSTORMING PAGE

(Yes, it's okay to write in this book!)

CHAPTER 6

PROVEN HEADLINE: "THE LAZY MAN'S WAY TO RICHES"

VARIATIONS FOR SPECIFIC BUSINESSES	
Ceramic Tile Contractor	The Lazy Homeowner's Way to Beautiful Floors and Counters
Limo Service	The Lazy Person's Way to Get Around Town
Restaurant Meals Delivery Service	The Lazy Cook's Way to Serve a Great Dinner
Salon and Spa	The Lazy Woman's Way to Look Absolutely Ravishing
Lawn Mowing and Hedge Trimming Service	The Lazy Homeowner's Way to Keep Your Lawn in Perfect Condition
Traveling Massage Therapist	The Lazy Person's Way to Relax Completely
Stop Smoking Program	The Lazy Smoker's Way to Quit – Permanently
Computer Instructor	The Lazy Person's Way to Computer Mastery

■ ■ ■

MORE VARIATIONS FOR SPECIFIC BUSINESSES	
Headhunter	The Lazy Executive's Way to Get a Great New Job
Housepainter	The Lazy Homeowner's Way to Get Your House Painted
Roof Repair	The Lazy Homeowner's Way to Get Your Roof Repaired
Self-Storage	The Lazy Person's Way to Deal With "Too Much Stuff"
Tour Bus Company	The Lazy Traveler's Way to Go on Vacation
Security Systems Installer	The Lazy Person's Way to Protect Your Home

HINTS ABOUT USING THIS HEADLINE

When people have too many things to do and not enough time to do them, <u>everything</u> seems like a lot of work — even if it isn't really. Many people feel "lazy" when in reality, they're just time-pressured. You can take advantage of this incorrect perception by presenting your service as the "lazy person's way" to do something — even if, in reality, what you're really doing is simply saving your customers precious time.

HOW TO ADAPT THIS HEADLINE TO YOUR BUSINESS — "THE LAZY (NAME YOUR PROSPECT)'S WAY TO (CONDITION, GOAL OR END RESULT YOUR PROSPECTS WANT, THAT YOU CAN PROVIDE FOR THEM)"

26

HEADLINE BRAINSTORMING PAGE

(Yes, it's okay to write in this book!)

HEADLINE BRAINSTORMING PAGE

(Yes, it's okay to write in this book!)

CHAPTER 7

PROVEN HEADLINE: "DO YOU MAKE THESE MISTAKES IN ENGLISH?"

VARIATIONS FOR SPECIFIC BUSINESSES	
Computer Training Business	Do You Make These Computer Mistakes?
Insurance Company	Are You Making Any of These Financial Mistakes?
Web Marketing Consultant	Do You Make These Web Marketing Mistakes?
Quick Oil-Change Service	Can You Spot These Auto Maintenance Mistakes?
Swimming Instructor	Do You Make These Common Swimming Mistakes?
Estate Planning Attorneys	Is Your Estate Vulnerable Because of These 7 Common Mistakes?
Speed Reading Instructor	Do You Make These Reading Mistakes?
Dry Cleaner	Do You Make These Apparel-Care Mistakes?
Home Remodeler	Do You Make These Home Maintenance Mistakes?

MORE VARIATIONS FOR SPECIFIC BUSINESSES	
Headhunter	Do You Make These Career-Damaging Mistakes?
Management Consultant	Do You Make These Management Mistakes?
Trade Show Display Company	Do You Make These Trade Show Mistakes?
Martial Arts School	Do You Make These Self-Defense Mistakes?
Plumber	Do You Make These Plumbing Mistakes?
Wedding Planner	Will You Make These Wedding Mistakes?

HINTS ABOUT USING THIS HEADLINE

People worry about making mistakes. Even risk-takers, who know their lives will never be mistake-free, would like to make fewer mistakes if possible. Everyone would like to avoid mistakes if they could. So when you set up your ad with a headline like this, bring up mistakes in your copy and point out how buying from you can help your prospect prevent or eliminate these mistakes.

HOW TO ADAPT THIS HEADLINE TO YOUR BUSINESS — "DO YOU MAKE THESE (TYPE OF SERVICE YOU PROVIDE) MISTAKES?"

OR

"CAN YOU SPOT THESE (NUMBER OF) COMMON (TYPE OF SERVICE YOU PROVIDE) MISTAKES?"

HEADLINE BRAINSTORMING PAGE

(Yes, it's okay to write in this book!)

_____

_____

_____

_____

_____

_____

_____

_____

_____

_____

_____

_____

_____

HEADLINE BRAINSTORMING PAGE

(Yes, it's okay to write in this book!)

CHAPTER 8

PROVEN HEADLINE: "SPEAK SPANISH LIKE A DIPLOMAT"

VARIATIONS FOR SPECIFIC BUSINESSES	
Music Teacher	Play Guitar Like A Rock Star
Ski Instructor	Ski Like An Olympic Champion
Trendy Night Club	Party Like A Jet-Setter
Cooking School	Prepare Meals Like A Paris Chef
Plastic Surgeon	Look Like A Million Dollars
Golf Instructor	Play Golf Like A PGA Pro
Baseball Camp	Play Ball Like A World Series Champion
Public Speaking Instructor	Speak Like A Pro
Dance Instructor	Dance With The Best Of Them
Flying Instructor	Fly Planes Like An Expert
Riding Academy	Ride Like A Champion

HINTS ABOUT USING THIS HEADLINE

You may recall seeing this headline in an airline magazine. It was written by my friend Don Hauptman, who is also a master copywriter. The ad ran for decades and made millions of dollars for the advertiser, who was selling an audiotape language instruction program.

The headline works because it appeals to the basic human urge for self-improvement. The reason it's so effective is that, in just a few words, it invites (or challenges) readers to perform an activity at the level of a world-class master — with the original, speaking Spanish as well as a diplomat.

HOW TO ADAPT THIS HEADLINE TO YOUR BUSINESS — " (DO ACTIVITY) LIKE (WORLD-CLASS PRACTIONER OF THIS ACTIVITY) ."

HEADLINE BRAINSTORMING PAGE

(Yes, it's okay to write in this book!)

HEADLINE BRAINSTORMING PAGE

(Yes, it's okay to write in this book!)

CHAPTER 9

PROVEN HEADLINE: "IF YOU'RE <u>OUT</u> OF THE MARKET NOW, YOU'LL <u>HATE</u> YOURSELF LATER"

VARIATIONS FOR SPECIFIC BUSINESSES	
High-Speed Internet Provider	If You <u>Don't</u> Get Broadband Now, You'll <u>Hate</u> Yourself Later
Dance Studio	If You <u>Don't</u> Learn to Dance Now, You'll <u>Hate</u> Yourself Later
Bank	If You <u>Don't</u> Start Saving Now, You'll <u>Hate</u> Yourself Later
Furniture Re-upholsterer	If You <u>Don't</u> Re-Upholster Your Furniture Now, You'll <u>Hate</u> Yourself Later
Security Systems Installer	If You <u>Don't</u> Protect Your Home Now, You'll <u>Hate</u> Yourself Later
Safari Tour Company	If You <u>Don't</u> Take A Safari While You Still Can, You'll <u>Hate</u> Yourself Later
Chiropractor	If You <u>Don't</u> Fix Your Back Problem Now, You'll <u>Hate</u> Yourself Later

■   ■   ■

MORE VARIATIONS FOR SPECIFIC BUSINESSES	
Financial Planner	If You <u>Don't</u> Plan For Your Retirement Now, You'll <u>Hate</u> Yourself Later
Hair Replacement Specialist	If You <u>Don't</u> Turn Your Hair Problem Around Now, You'll <u>Hate</u> Yourself Later
Health Club	If You <u>Don't</u> Get In Shape Now, You'll <u>Hate</u> Yourself Later
Ceramic Tile Contractor	If You <u>Don't</u> Replace Your Old Tile Now, You'll <u>Hate</u> Yourself Later
Dentist	If You <u>Don't</u> Take Care of That Toothache Now, You'll <u>Hate</u> Yourself Later
Accountant	If You <u>Don't</u> Handle Your IRS Problem Now, You'll <u>Hate</u> Yourself Later
Tire Store	If You <u>Don't</u> Get New Tires Now, You'll <u>Hate</u> Yourself Later
Photographer	If You <u>Don't</u> Get a Family Portrait Now, You'll <u>Hate</u> Yourself Later

HINTS ABOUT USING THIS HEADLINE

Another Don Hauptman classic headline. This was written to get subscribers for an investment newsletter. It plays on the fear of missing a fleeting opportunity now, and the added fear of feeling regret about it later. Since nearly everyone regrets failing to act on some opportunity in the past, this kind of headline rings true with most people when they read it.

■ ■ ■

The key to make this headline work is to decide what you offer as a product or service that a buyer could later see as a missed opportunity later on if the buyer fails to take advantage of it now — and plug that into the headline.

Then be sure to follow up in your copy. For example, with the first variation, for a security system installer (**If You <u>Don't</u> Protect Your Home Now, You'll <u>Hate</u> Yourself Later**), you would talk about the terror and heartbreak of having your home invaded — and how you could have prevented that if you had installed a home security system beforehand.

HOW TO ADAPT THIS HEADLINE TO YOUR BUSINESS — "IF YOU <u>(DON'T TAKE ADVANTAGE OF THIS OPPORTUNITY YOUR COMPANY PROVIDES),</u> YOU'LL <u>HATE</u> YOURSELF LATER."

HEADLINE BRAINSTORMING PAGE

(Yes, it's okay to write in this book!)

_____

_____

_____

_____

_____

_____

_____

_____

_____

_____

_____

_____

_____

CHAPTER 10

PROVEN HEADLINE: "DO YOU RECOGNIZE THE 7
EARLY WARNING SIGNS OF HIGH BLOOD PRESSURE?"

VARIATIONS FOR SPECIFIC BUSINESSES	
Roof Repair	Do You Recognize The 7 Early Warning Signs Of A Leaky Roof?
Management Consultant	Do You Recognize The 7 Early Warning Signs Of Employee Insurrection?
Candy Store	Do You Recognize The 7 Early Warning Signs Of Candy Deprivation?
Cruise Line	Do You Recognize The 7 Early Warning Signs Of Workaday Stress?
Tire Store	Do You Recognize The 7 Early Warning Signs Of Sudden Tire Failure?
Therapist	Do You Recognize The 7 Early Warning Signs Of An Emotional Breakdown?
Accountant	Do You Recognize The 7 Early Warning Signs Of Embezzlement?

MORE VARIATIONS FOR SPECIFIC BUSINESSES	
Personal Trainer	Do You Recognize The 7 Early Warning Signs Of "Permanent Pot-Belly?"
Wedding Planner	Do You Recognize The 7 Early Warning Signs Of Potential Wedding Crisis?
Professional Organizer	Do You Recognize The 7 Early Warning Signs Of Gridlock Clutter?
Office Furniture Store	Do You Recognize The 7 Early Warning Signs Of Outgrowing Your Office Furniture?
Publicist	Do You Recognize The 7 Early Warning Signs Of An Impending PR Crisis?
Copier Sales	Do You Recognize The 7 Early Warning Signs Of A Copier Breakdown?

HINTS ABOUT USING THIS HEADLINE

Here's where having some experience in your business really comes in handy. You probably know of a lot of the problems, frustrations, glitches and all-around hassles that lead people to seek you out. It's up to you name them and call them "early warning signs." Of course, you want them to be crux of your copy. Be sure to end the copy with a call to action.

This headline works so well because people are often nervous about trouble ahead, and will be drawn into an ad with a headline like this to see if any of the warning signs apply in their situation. Then, it's up to you to make it easy and safe for them to contact you.

HOW TO ADAPT THIS HEADLINE TO YOUR BUSINESS — "DO YOUR RECOGNIZE THE 7 EARLY WARNING SIGNS OF (PROBLEM THAT YOU SOLVE) ?"

HEADLINE BRAINSTORMING PAGE

(Yes, it's okay to write in this book!)

CHAPTER 11

PROVEN HEADLINE: "THE MOST COMFORTABLE SHOES YOU'VE EVER WORN OR YOUR MONEY BACK"

VARIATIONS FOR SPECIFIC BUSINESSES	
Razor Manufacturer	The Smoothest Shave You've Ever Had or Your Money Back
Office Supply Store	Best Quality Office Supplies at the Lowest Prices or Your Money Back
Driving School	The Most Patient Driving Instructors In Town or Your Money Back
Jewelry Store	The Most Elegant Jewelry You've Ever Seen or Your Money Back
Riding Academy	You'll Feel Totally at Home on Our Horses or Your First Lesson's Free
Dry Cleaners	The Best Care Your Clothes Have Ever Received Or Your Money Back
Trade Show Display Company	The Most Attractive Tradeshow Display You've Ever Seen or Your Money Back

MORE VARIATIONS FOR SPECIFIC BUSINESSES	
Home Entertainment Store	The Most Awesome Home Theatre You've Ever Experienced, Or Your Money Back
Singing Telegram Company	The Most Memorable Message Ever Delivered On Your Behalf, Or Your Money Back
Time Management Expert	The Most Useful Time-Saving Tips You've Ever Seen, Or Your Money Back
Denture Adhesive	You Won't Even Realize You're Wearing Dentures, Or Your Money Back
Limo Service	The Smoothest Ride You've Ever Taken, Or Your Money Back

HINTS ABOUT USING THIS HEADLINE

You can use this headline when you have the kind of business where you can offer your customers a money-back guarantee, and you have the confidence to do so. Then, you need to have a specific, out-of-the-ordinary claim you can make — "the most comfortable shoes you've ever worn," "the most elegant jewelry you've ever seen," — that most of your current customers agree with.

If you already offer a money-back guarantee, why not take advantage of it in your advertising? Most businesses that do end up with far more additional sales than refund requests.

HOW TO ADAPT THIS HEADLINE TO YOUR BUSINESS — "THE (MAKE A BOLD CLAIM THAT YOU CAN LIVE UP TO) OR YOUR MONEY BACK."

HEADLINE BRAINSTORMING PAGE

(Yes, it's okay to write in this book!)

CHAPTER 12

PROVEN HEADLINE: "SEE HOW EASILY YOU CAN LEARN TO DANCE THIS NEW WAY"

VARIATIONS FOR SPECIFIC BUSINESSES	
Publicist	See How Easily You Can Get Publicity For Your Business
Time Management Expert	See How Easily You Can Get More Done This New Way
Flying Instructor	See How Easily You Can Learn To Fly This New Way
Architect	See How Easily You Can Design Your New Home With Our Help
Health Food Store	See How Easily You Can Have A Delicious, Healthier Diet
Hair Replacement Specialist	See How Easily You Can Have A Full Head Of Hair
Snowmobile Dealer	See How Easily You Can Cruise Through Mountain Snows

MORE VARIATIONS FOR SPECIFIC BUSINESSES	
Housepainter	See How Easily You Can Get Your House Painted
Photographer	See How Easily You Can Get Beautiful Portraits Made
Personal Trainer	See How Easily You Can Get In Shape With My Help
Safari Tour Company	See How Easily You Can Take A Safari
Persian Rug Store	See How Easily You Can Own A Persian Rug
Acupuncturist	See How Easily You Can Try Acupuncture
Swimming Instructor	See How Easily You Can Learn To Swim
Speed Reading Instructor	See How Easily You Can Learn Speed Reading This New Way
Web Designer	See How Easily You Can Have A Great Web Site

HINTS ABOUT USING THIS HEADLINE

Everything in life is a combination of hard and easy. What's different is the proportions. Some things are almost all easy, and other things have very few easy aspects.

When you're selling with a headline, do yourself a favor (make it easy on yourself) and focus on what's easy about doing business with you. Then expand on it in your copy.

The original proven headline was used to successfully sell Arthur Murray home-study dance courses in the 1920s.

HOW TO ADAPT THIS HEADLINE TO YOUR BUSINESS — "SEE HOW EASILY YOU CAN (RESULT YOU PROVIDE) (HOW YOU PROVIDE IT: "THIS NEW WAY," "WITH MY HELP," ETC.)."

HEADLINE BRAINSTORMING PAGE

(Yes, it's okay to write in this book!)

CHAPTER 13

PROVEN HEADLINE: "YOU DON'T HAVE TO BE RICH TO RETIRE ON A GUARANTEED INCOME FOR LIFE"

VARIATIONS FOR SPECIFIC BUSINESSES	
Hotel	You Don't Have to Be Famous to Get the "Star Treatment" at Our Hotel
Clothing Store	You Don't Have to Be Model-Thin to Look Absolutely Gorgeous In Our Clothes
Public Speaking Instructor	You Don't Need Nerves of Steel to Hold an Audience Spellbound
Home Remodeler	You Don't Need a Huge Budget to Have Your Home Beautifully Remodeled
Computer Instructor	You Don't Need a Genius I.Q. to Become a Whiz at Your Computer
Cosmetic Dentist	You Don't Need Perfect Genes to Have a Movie-Star Smile
Sculptor	You Don't Need a Degree in Fine Arts to Have Museum-Quality Sculpture in Your Home

MORE VARIATIONS FOR SPECIFIC BUSINESSES	
Payroll Service	You Don't Need a Staff Accountant to Get Your Payroll Handled Professionally for You
Locksmith	You Don't Need to Work for the CIA to Get Your Locks Open Without a Key

HINTS ABOUT USING THIS HEADLINE

Here again, it really pays to know how your customers think. In the proven headline, there's some very smart psychology. Most people think you need to have loads of money to get a guaranteed income for life, while in fact there are other legitimate, reliable ways to achieve the same goal.

When you're using this headline, ask yourself: What mental barriers do prospects erect — falsely — to disqualify themselves from doing business with you? Knock down those barriers in this headline, and you'll greatly broaden your market.

HOW TO ADAPT THIS HEADLINE TO YOUR BUSINESS — "YOU DON'T NEED/HAVE TO (WHAT PEOPLE THINK THEY NEED, AS A PREREQUISITE) TO (GET A DESIRED RESULT THAT YOU CAN PROVIDE, THAT PEOPLE THOUGHT THEY COULDN'T GET) ."

HEADLINE BRAINSTORMING PAGE

(Yes, it's okay to write in this book!)

_____

_____

_____

_____

_____

_____

_____

_____

_____

_____

_____

_____

_____

HEADLINE BRAINSTORMING PAGE

(Yes, it's okay to write in this book!)

CHAPTER 14

PROVEN HEADLINE: "WHAT'S NEW IN
SUMMER SANDWICHES?"

VARIATIONS FOR SPECIFIC BUSINESSES	
Bicycle Shop	What's New in Mountain Bikes?
Daycare Center	What's New in Daycare?
Office Rentals	What's New in Furnished Offices?
Construction Equipment Dealer	What's New in Construction Equipment?
Financial Planner	What's New in Financial Planning?
Tour Bus Company	What's New in Group Tours?
Singing Telegram Company	What's New in Party Surprises?
Copier Sales	What's New in Office Copiers?
Persian Carpet Store	What's New in Persian Carpets?

MORE VARIATIONS FOR SPECIFIC BUSINESSES	
Advertising Specialties	What's New in Advertising Specialties?
Self-Storage	What's New in Self-Storage?
Home Entertainment	What's New in High-Definition TV?

HINTS ABOUT USING THIS HEADLINE

It's deceptively easy. Remember to look at your business from your customer's point of view, and not from your own.

Here's why: You have an in-depth technical knowledge that your customers don't have — and don't want to have. Say you were in the telephone equipment business. "What's New In RJ11 Plugs?" might be fascinating to you, but real boring to your customers. "What's New in Digital Cordless Phones?" — the part of what you sell that customers see and care about — will work much better.

HOW TO ADAPT THIS HEADLINE TO YOUR BUSINESS — "WHAT'S NEW IN (SOMETHING YOUR CUSTOMER BUYS FROM YOU, IS FAMILIAR WITH AND INTERESTED IN) ?"

HEADLINE BRAINSTORMING PAGE

(Yes, it's okay to write in this book!)

HEADLINE BRAINSTORMING PAGE

(Yes, it's okay to write in this book!)

CHAPTER 15

PROVEN HEADLINE: "10 WAYS TO BEAT THE HIGH COST OF LIVING"

VARIATIONS FOR SPECIFIC BUSINESSES	
Financial Advisor	10 Ways to Build a Secure Financial Future
Personal Trainer	10 Ways to Stay in Tip-Top Shape
Quick Oil-Change Service	10 Ways to Keep Your Car Running Smoothly
Caterers	10 Ways to Throw a Successful Party
Web Hosting Company	10 Ways to Build an Awesome Web Site
Bed and Breakfast	10 Ways to Lower Stress and Enjoy Yourself Again
Headhunter	10 Ways to Get the Job You've Always Dreamed Of
Real Estate Agent	10 Ways to Find the Home That's Just Right for You
Professional Organizer	10 Ways to Be Perfectly Organized

■ ■ ■

MORE VARIATIONS FOR SPECIFIC BUSINESSES	
Camera Store	10 Ways to Take Great Pictures
Personal Coach	10 Ways to Live the Life You've Always Dreamed Of
Wedding Planner	10 Ways to Have The Most Wonderful Wedding Imaginable
Limo Service	10 Ways to Have an Awesome Night on the Town
Dentist	10 Ways to Have a Great Smile
Grocery Store	10 Ways to Serve More Delicious, Nutritious Meals

HINTS ABOUT USING THIS HEADLINE

Here's where you can cash in on all your years of experience and accumulated knowledge. For example, if you're a financial planner, you're used to giving clients options about how to build financial security. The key to using this knowledge successfully in an ad with a headline like this is to spell it out plainly, concisely and specifically — and keep it interesting. That will make people want to call you.

The phrase "he knows what he's talking about" (and "she knows what she's talking about") are shorthand for "this person is competent and worth doing business with." This headline is a way to get in that category. Of course, you need to deliver in your copy, by providing really outstanding information, well written and easy to read. The benefits of running an ad demonstrating your knowledge clearly and accessibly, you instantly catapult your status to "someone who knows what they're talking about."

Be sure at the end to include a clear call to action. People need to be led to take the action you want them to take.

HOW TO ADAPT THIS HEADLINE TO YOUR BUSINESS — "10 WAYS TO (ACTION THAT OBVIOUSLY LEADS TO AN END RESULT YOU CAN HELP CLIENTS OR CUSTOMERS CREATE, OR CONDITION THAT PEOPLE WOULD RATHER BE IN THAN THE ONE THEY'RE IN NOW)."

HEADLINE BRAINSTORMING PAGE

(Yes, it's okay to write in this book!)

CHAPTER 16

PROVEN HEADLINE: "NEW CONCEPT IN WEIGHT CONTROL"

VARIATIONS FOR SPECIFIC BUSINESSES	
Health Food Store	New Concept in Nutrition
Kitchen Remodeler	New Concept in Kitchen Design
Financial Advisor	New Concept in Wealth Preservation
Cruise Line	New Concept in Unforgettable Vacations
Camera Store	New Concept in Photography
Limo Service	New Concept in Time Management
Stop-Smoking Program	New Concept in Quitting Smoking
Wedding Planner	New Concept in Wedding Planning
Martial Arts	New Concept in Self-Defense
Luggage Store	New Concept in Stress-Free Travel
Traveling Massage Therapist	New Concept in Stress Reduction

MORE VARIATIONS FOR SPECIFIC BUSINESSES	
Personal Coach	New Concept in Goal Achievement
Razor Manufacturer	New Concept in Shaving
Web Hosting Company	New Concept in Web Hosting
Hair Replacement Specialist	New Concept in Hair Replacement
Restaurant Meals Delivery Service	New Concept in Gourmet Dining
Driving School	New Concept in Learning to Drive
Bicycle Shop	New Concept in Mountain Biking
Speed Reading Instructor	New Concept in Speed Reading
Tire Store	New Concept in Driving Comfort

HINTS ABOUT USING THIS HEADLINE

When you use this headline, you're making a promise — so in your copy, make sure you deliver on your promise.

Three ways you can do that:

- Announce a new product or service

- Describe a unique feature of a product, or a unique way you deliver your service, or

■ ■ ■

■ Use your creativity in some other way to discover and explain something new about what you offer your customers.

Make sure whatever you say will not only come across as *new*, but also *convey value and benefit* to your customer.

HOW TO ADAPT THIS HEADLINE TO YOUR BUSINESS — "NEW CONCEPT IN (SOMETHING THAT A GOOD PROSPECT FOR YOUR BUSINESS WILL INSTANTLY RECOGNIZE AND WANT TO KNOW MORE ABOUT) ."

HEADLINE BRAINSTORMING PAGE

(Yes, it's okay to write in this book!)

_____

_____

_____

_____

_____

_____

_____

_____

_____

_____

_____

_____

CHAPTER 17

PROVEN HEADLINE: "THE SECRET OF MAKING PEOPLE LIKE YOU"

VARIATIONS FOR SPECIFIC BUSINESSES	
Discount Carpet Store	The Secret of Luxurious Carpets on a Budget
Security Systems Installer	The Secret of Feeling Safe at Home
Chiropractor	The Secret of Feeling Great Naturally
Dry Cleaner	The Secret of Making Your Clothes Last Longer
Florist	The Secret of Making Up After a Fight
Computer Instructor	The Secret of Mastering Your Computer
Beauty Salon	The Secret of Looking Absolutely Gorgeous
Bank	The Secret of Getting Your Loan Approved
Dentist	The Secret of a Beautiful Smile
Veterinarian	The Secret of Having Healthy Pets
Insurance Company	The Secret of a Worry-Free Retirement

MORE VARIATIONS FOR SPECIFIC BUSINESSES	
Management Consultant	The Secret of a Happy Workplace
Professional Organizer	The Secret of Staying Organized
Self-Storage	The Secret of Having Enough Space
Financial Planner	The Secret of Financial Peace of Mind
Advertising Specialties	The Secret of Making Customers Remember You
Babysitting Service	The Secret of Going Out When You Have Children
Estate Planning Attorney	The Secret of Avoiding Unnecessary Taxes
Ceramic Tile Contractor	The Secret of Beautiful Floors
Tire Store	New Concept in Driving Comfort

HINTS ABOUT USING THIS HEADLINE

A lot of businesspeople know things from years of experience that their customers don't know. Though this information is common knowledge to the businessperson, it seems like a secret to the customer who has never heard it before.

The trick to using this information in a headline is to convert it into a benefit for your prospects. Then, work backwards from the benefit in your copy to explaining the secret, and inviting your prospect to contact you, or to buy right away.

■   ■   ■

Example: Bankers know perfectly well which loans they will approve, and why. But very few bank customers know. Why? Because the bankers haven't told them.

So a headline "The Secrets of Getting Your Loan Approved," followed by a friendly, conversational explanation of what to do to maximize your chances of approval, and then followed by an invitation to come into the bank, would bring new customers.

How To Adapt This Headline To Your Business — "The Secret of (An Outcome Your Customers Would Want, That You Can Deliver) ."

HEADLINE BRAINSTORMING PAGE

(Yes, it's okay to write in this book!)

CHAPTER 18

PROVEN HEADLINE: "HOW TO WIN FRIENDS AND INFLUENCE PEOPLE"

VARIATIONS FOR SPECIFIC BUSINESSES	
Hypnotherapist	How to Change Habits and Get Results
Bank	How to Save Money and Retire Rich
Health Food Store	How to Change Your Food and Feel Great!
Landscaping Service	How to Design Your Lawn So You Get Compliments
Cosmetic Dentist	How to Change Your Smile and Become More Attractive
Dance Studio	How to Dance Comfortably and Become More Popular
Hair Replacement Specialist	How to Have More Hair and Be More Attractive
Camera Store	How to Take Great Pictures and Be Proud of Them!

MORE VARIATIONS FOR SPECIFIC BUSINESSES	
Kitchen Remodeler	How to Change Your Kitchen and Enjoy Your Home More
Yoga Instructor	How to Loosen Up and Relax!
Quick Oil-Change Service	How to Save Time and Make Your Car Last Longer
Tire Store	How to Drive Safely and Ride Comfortably
Safari Tour Company	How to Have an Exciting Vacation and Make Your Friends Envious
Martial Arts School	How to Stay Fit and Protect Yourself
Stop-Smoking Program	How to Kick the Habit and Feel Great
Luggage Store	How to Be Stylish and Travel in Comfort
Candy Store	How to Have Fun and Satisfy Cravings
Time Management Expert	How to Save Time and Get Things Done
Salon and Spa	How to Totally Relax and Feel Great
Headhunter	How to Get a Better Job and Make More Money

HINTS ABOUT USING THIS HEADLINE

Besides being the title for Dale Carnegie's best-selling book, "How to Win Friends and Influence People" was also the headline for a very successful direct-response ad that sold the book by mail-order.

The book was successful, certainly, because of the quality and value of the content. But the title/headline itself is pure genius. Here's why: It carries a <u>triple</u> whammy:

1) It has benefit number 1 after "How to"

2) It has benefit number 2 after "and"

3) And, there is a very subtle implied cause-and-effect relationship between benefit number 1 and benefit number 2. That is, it <u>seems</u> like if you achieve the first benefit — having friends — then you will automatically achieve the second benefit — influencing people.

Never mind whether this is logical or not. (There are plenty of people who have friends who aren't all that influential.) The perception of cause-and-effect comes from the structure of the words, not from any real-world relationship between the words.

However, for maximum credibility, strive to include benefits in your headline that really <u>do</u> have a legitimate cause-and-effect relationship in the real world. Notice how I did that in the variation headlines, above.

HOW TO ADAPT THIS HEADLINE TO YOUR BUSINESS — "HOW TO <u>(FIRST BENEFIT)</u> TO <u>(SECOND BENEFIT)</u>."

HEADLINE BRAINSTORMING PAGE

(Yes, it's okay to write in this book!)

_____

_____

_____

_____

_____

_____

_____

_____

_____

_____

_____

_____

_____

CHAPTER 19

PROVEN HEADLINE: "WHY SOME PEOPLE ALMOST
ALWAYS MAKE MONEY IN THE STOCK MARKET"

VARIATIONS FOR SPECIFIC BUSINESSES	
Snowmobile Dealer	Why Some People Almost Always Have More Fun in the Winter
Publicist	Why Some Businesses Get Positive Publicity Almost All the Time
Management Consultant	Why Some Companies Are Almost Always More Productive
Daycare Center	Why Some Parents Almost Always Have Free Time
Clothing Store	Why Some People Almost Always Look Fashionable
Personal Trainer	Why Some People Almost Always Have High Energy
Swimming Instructor	Why Some People Almost Always Have More Fun at the Beach

MORE VARIATIONS FOR SPECIFIC BUSINESSES

Office Supply Store	Why Some Businesses Almost Never Run Out of Office Supplies
Speed Reading Instructor	Why Some People Are Almost Always Caught Up on Their Reading
Web Designer	Why Some Web Sites Are Almost Always More Profitable
Real Estate Agent	Why Some People Are Almost Always Happier With Where They Live
Traveling Massage Therapist	Why Some People Almost Always Look Relaxed
Persian Rug Dealer	Why Some People Are Almost Always Proud of Their Floors
Payroll Service	Why Some Businesses Almost Never Have Payroll Problems
Headhunter	Why Some People Almost Never Have a Bad Day at Work
Bed and Breakfast	Why Some People Are Almost Always Relaxed After the Weekend
Copier Sales	Why Some Businesses Almost Never Have Problems With Their Copiers
Health Food Store	Why Some People Feel Great Almost All the Time

■ ■ ■

MORE VARIATIONS FOR SPECIFIC BUSINESSES	
Luxury Car Dealer	Why Some People Almost Always Enjoy Driving
Estate Planning Attorney	Why Some People Almost Always Feel Secure About Their Net Worth

HINTS ABOUT USING THIS HEADLINE

The reason this headline was so successful is that it didn't make a blanket statement. It didn't say: Why **All** People **Always** Make Money In the Stock Market. It didn't even say: Why Some People **Always** Make Money in the Stock Market.

What it said was, "Why **Some** People **Almost** Always Make Money in the Stock Market." Now, that's interesting. And plausible. Because by admitting that even the most fortunate or clever investor among us doesn't live in a perfect world, this headline gains in credibility and power to arouse curiosity.

When you use a variation of this headline, remember how this hedging adds to credibility in the headline. What you should do is find a non-fatal flaw in the product or service you provide, or the results you deliver, to use in your copy. You'll need that to explain why you say "almost always" (or "almost never") instead of "always" (or "never.")

Example: For the Daycare Center headline, it would be totally unbelievable to a parent to believe that there are any parents who <u>always</u> have free time, even if there are some who do. But parents who have a place to drop off their kids could have more free time, and it's even

79

possible that they could <u>almost always</u> have some free time. So you would want to mention the "almost always" in the headline, to show empathy, and maintain rapport and credibility.

How To Adapt This Headline To Your Business — "Why Some <u>(Describe Your Prospects)</u> Almost Always <u>(Do or Achieve Something Your Prospects Want More Of)</u> ."

HEADLINE BRAINSTORMING PAGE

(Yes, it's okay to write in this book!)

_____

_____

_____

_____

_____

_____

_____

_____

_____

_____

_____

_____

_____

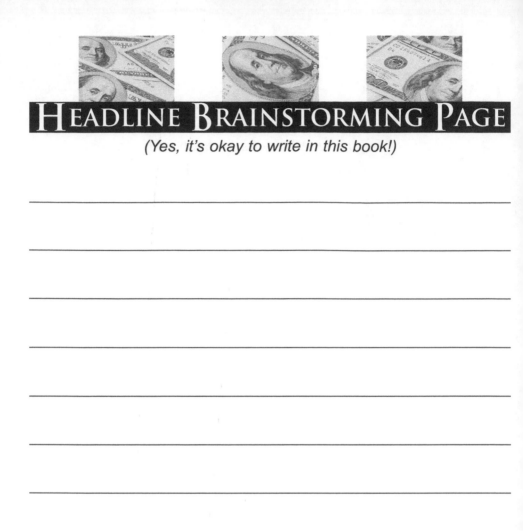

HEADLINE BRAINSTORMING PAGE

(Yes, it's okay to write in this book!)

CHAPTER 20

PROVEN HEADLINE: "FIVE FAMILIAR SKIN TROUBLES — WHICH DO YOU WANT TO OVERCOME?"

VARIATIONS FOR SPECIFIC BUSINESSES	
Dry Cleaner	Five Common Clothing Stains – Which Ones Do You Want to Get Rid of?
Housepainter	Five Familiar Problems with Walls and Ceilings – Which Ones Do You Want to Overcome?
Financial Planner	Five Common Financial Problems – Which Ones Do You Want to Overcome?
Headhunter	Five Familiar Career Problems – Which Ones Do You Want to Overcome?
Chiropractor	Five Familiar Back Problems – Which Ones Do You Want to Fix?
Dentist	Five Problems People Have With Their Teeth – Which Ones Do You Want to Overcome?
Caterer	Five Familiar Party Planning Problems – Which Ones Do You Want to Overcome?

MORE VARIATIONS FOR SPECIFIC BUSINESSES

Computer Training Business	Five Problems That Plague Microsoft Office Users – Which Ones Do You Want to Overcome?
Payroll Service	Five Familiar Payroll Problems – Which Ones Do You Want to Overcome?
Web Designer	Five Familiar Web Site Problems – Which Ones Do You Want to Overcome?
Professional Organizer	Five Familiar Clutter Problems – Which Ones Do You Want to Overcome?
Security System Installer	Five Familiar Home Security Problems – Which Ones Do You Want to Overcome?
Riding Academy	Five Familiar Equestrian Problems – Which Ones Do You Want to Overcome?
Landscaping Service	Five Familiar Lawn Problems – Which Ones Do You Want to Overcome?
Hair Replacement Specialist	Five Problems Men with Thinning Hair Have – Which Ones Do You Want to Solve?
Accountant	Five Familiar Tax Problems – Which Ones Do You Want to Overcome?
Martial Arts School	Five Familiar Self-Defense Problems – Which Ones Do You Want to Solve?
Copier Sales	Five Familiar Photocopier Problems – Which Ones Do You Want to Overcome?
Quick Oil-Change Service	Five Familiar Car Maintenance Problems – Which Ones Do You Want to Avoid

■   ■   ■

HINTS ABOUT USING THIS HEADLINE

You know from experience which problems customers typically bring to you — or, maybe more to the point, which problems force customers to realize they can't put off seeing you any longer.

When you write your copy, write about problems your customers are already familiar with. This is not the time to educate prospects about new problems. Your goal here is to remind them of what they already know, so their intensified awareness will lead them to take action — namely, doing business with you.

HOW TO ADAPT THIS HEADLINE TO YOUR BUSINESS — "FIVE FAMILIAR _____ PROBLEMS — WHICH ONES DO YOU WANT TO OVERCOME?"

HEADLINE BRAINSTORMING PAGE

(Yes, it's okay to write in this book!)

BONUS #1

50 MORE KILLER HEADLINES YOU CAN USE FOR YOUR BUSINESS

In this Bonus, you get 50 more high-impact headlines you can easily adapt to your business. Here, you get the headlines and the template only. You can use what you've learned from the 297 variations in the first 20 chapters to adapt any of these headlines to your business.

1. NOW, HAVE THE LUXURY AND COMFORT OF A 100% SILK SUIT YOU CAN AFFORD!

Now, Have The (describe benefits) Of A (describe what you sell that seems more expensive than it is) That You Can Afford!

2. RATTAN THAT LOOKS EXPENSIVE AND IS WONDERFULLY COMFORTABLE.

(What you sell at a comparatively low price) That Looks Expensive And Is Wonderfully Comfortable.

3. OUR SOLID HARD ROCK MAPLE IS RUGGEDLY BUILT AND HONEY TONED.

Our (description of product) Is (first benefit) And (second benefit).

4. CUT YOUR GRASS QUICKLY AND EASILY WITH THE WORLD'S FIRST <u>SAFE</u> POWER MOWER.

(<u>Task your product accomplishes</u>) Quickly And Easily With (<u>benefit statement that includes description of your product</u>).

5. THEY LOOK LIKE WOOL, THEY FEEL LIKE WOOL, BUT THEY'LL WEAR 5 TIMES AS LONG.

They LOOK Like (<u>more expensive material</u>), They FEEL Like (<u>more expensive material</u>), But They'll (<u>benefit statement about how your product will out-perform the product made with the more expensive material</u>).

6. HOW MEDICATED CUTICURA HELPS CLEAR UP SKIN PROBLEMS

How (<u>your product's name</u>) Helps (<u>achieve your product's most desired beneficial result</u>)

7. YOU PRESS THE BUTTON — WE DO THE REST.

You (<u>take a simple action</u>) — We Do The Rest.

8. TO MEN WHO WANT TO QUIT WORK SOMEDAY

To (<u>prospects</u>) who want (<u>describe the prospects' dream that you can help them realize</u>)

9. WHAT EVERYBODY OUGHT TO KNOW... ABOUT THIS STOCK AND BOND BUSINESS

What Everybody Ought To Know... About This (<u>name of your business</u>) Business

10. How Fortune Came to John Jones

How (immense, desirable benefit) Came To (one of your customers)

Note: *This headline works when you have a true case study and a customer who gives you written permission to tell it.*

11. How a New Kind of Cream Makes the Skin Soft, Clear, Lovely — For Reasons That Every Woman Will Understand!

How a New Kind of (product you make) (produces a highly desirable result or set of results) — For Reasons That Every (describe your target customer) Will Understand!

12. Now You Can Have Sun-Ripened Oranges and Grapefruits Right Off The Trees!

Now You Can Have (appealing description of what you offer) (in the most appealing circumstances imaginable)!

13. Here Is A Method That Is Helping Thousands To Improve And Renew Their Vital Tone Of Youth!

Here is a Method That Is Helping (describe your customer group) to (describe the benefit(s) they are receiving)

14. You Can Laugh At Scraggly Lawns — If You Follow This Plan

You Can Laugh At (big problem or frustration your prospects have) — If You Follow This Plan

15. ARE YOU PREPARED TO PROFIT FROM A BOOM IN STOCK PRICES?

Are You Prepared To (<u>verb describing benefit</u>) From (<u>situation you can help prospect take advantage of</u>)?

16. LITTLE KNOWN WAYS TO LIFETIME PROFITS

Little Known Ways To (<u>benefit you provide</u>)

17. HOW TO STOP WORRYING AND START LIVING

How To Stop (<u>undesirable activity</u>) And Start (<u>desirable activity, which your prospect is able to enjoy because of the benefit you offer</u>)

18. 13 SURE-FIRE ROADS TO RICHES

13 Sure-Fire (<u>roads, paths, ways, etc. to a benefit you offer</u>)

19. WANT TO BE FINANCIALLY INDEPENDENT?

Want To Be (<u>beneficial condition you can provide for your prospect</u>)?

20. HOW TO ACHIEVE TOTAL FINANCIAL FREEDOM

How To Achieve (<u>describe desired achievement you can help your prospect attain</u>)

21. HOW TO BEAT THE IRS

How to (<u>defeat</u>) (<u>a feared enemy of your prospects</u>)

Note: This must relate to the solution or benefit you provide.

22. LEARN HOW TO ERASE BAD CREDIT.

Learn How To (<u>make a change you can help your prospects make</u>).

23. Land A Job In Two Days With New Method.

(Acquire a benefit) In (surprisingly short period of time) With New Method.

24. The Wrong Way And The Right Way To Buy A Used Car

The Wrong Way And The Right Way To (do something directly related to your business)

25. New Shampoo Leaves Your Hair Smoother — Easier To Manage

New (type of product you provide)(provides)(benefits your product offers)

26. How To Have A Cool, Quiet Bedroom — Even On Hot Nights

How To Have (describe what you can deliver) Even (describe condition in which your prospect believe what you offer is difficult or impossible to obtain)

27. You'll Never Drive A Dirty Car Again!

You'll Never (do an undesirable activity that you can help the prospect avoid doing) Again!

28. How To Get Rid Of An Inferiority Complex

How To Get Rid Of (Problem You Can Help Prospects Get Rid Of)

29. If You Are A Careful Driver, You Can Save Money On Car Insurance.

If You Are (describe the prospect you are looking for), You Can (make your offer to those prospects).

30. HOW TO DO YOUR CHRISTMAS SHOPPING IN 5 MINUTES
How To (<u>describe typically time-consuming activity</u>) In (<u>describe surprisingly short amount of time you can help your prospect do the activity in</u>)

31. HOW TO CUT FUEL BILLS
How To (<u>reduce or eliminate a pressing problem your prospect has</u>)

32. KEYS TO FITNESS AT ANY AGE — FOR MEN AND WOMEN
Keys To (<u>benefit you offer prospects</u>) — For (<u>describe your prospects</u>)

33. ARE YOU EMBARRASSED BY SMELLS IN YOUR HOME?
Are You Embarrassed By (<u>embarrassing problem you can solve for your prospects</u>)?

34. HERE'S A QUICK WAY TO BREAK UP A COLD
Here's A Quick Way To (<u>solve a problem for your prospects</u>)

35. HOW TO BEAT TENSION WITHOUT PILLS
How To (<u>solve a problem</u>) Without (<u>having to do some objectionable thing most people associate with solving the problem</u>)

36. HOW TO COLLECT FROM SOCIAL SECURITY AT ANY AGE
How To (<u>receive a benefit now that most people thought they couldn't receive under their present circumstances</u>)

37. IT CLEANS YOUR BREATH WHILE IT CLEANS YOUR TEETH
It (<u>provides one benefit</u>) While It (<u>provides a surprising, but related, other benefit</u>)

38. Quick Relief For Tired Eyes
Quick Relief For (<u>problem your prospect is experiencing</u>)

39. Right And Wrong Farming Methods — And Little Pointers That Will Increase Your Profits
Right And Wrong (<u>describe what your prospects do</u>) — And Little Pointers That Will (<u>describe a benefit you provide that your prospects want</u>)

40. Should You Invest In A Tax-Exempt Bond Fund?
Should You (<u>do something the prospect has probably been thinking about doing</u>)?

41. Own A Rembrandt For Only $7.95
Own A (<u>something normally expensive</u>) For Only (<u>a surprisingly low price</u>)

42. You're Never Too Old To Hear Better.
You're Never Too (<u>condition</u>) To (<u>do activity your prospects assume isn't possible to do in the condition you just described</u>).

43. How Investors Can Save 75% On Commissions This Year
How (<u>prospects</u>) Can (<u>achieve desirable benefit</u>) This Year

44. How To Live Better For Less
How To (<u>obtain benefit in surprising appealing or affordable way</u>)

45. When Doctors Have Headaches, What Do They Do?
When (<u>authorities</u>) have (<u>a problem related to their authority or specialty</u>), What Do They Do?

46. Don't Let Athlete's Foot "Lay You Up"

Don't Let (<u>problem-causing condition you solve for your prospects</u>) (<u>cause the problem</u>)

47. Check The Kind Of Body You Want

Check The Kind Of (<u>benefit you provide your prospects</u>) You Want

Note: *With a headline like this, you want to have a checklist of different types of bodies — or whatever it is that you can help your prospects obtain — in the copy of the ad itself*

48. Announcing... The New Edition Of The Encyclopedia That Makes It Fun To Learn Things

Announcing... The New (<u>describe the latest version of your product or service</u>) That (<u>describe a benefit of your product or service</u>)

49. New Cake-Improver Gets You Compliments Galore!

New (<u>product or service</u>) gets you (<u>benefit your prospect values</u>)

50. It's A Shame For You Not To Make Good Money — When These Men Do It So Easily

It's A Shame For You Not To (<u>achieve a goal you can help prospects achieve</u>) — When These (<u>describe people like your prospects</u>) Do It So Easily

BONUS #2

HOW TO DEVELOP A "HEADLINE CONSCIOUSNESS" THAT CAN MAKE YOU <u>MILLIONS</u>

E very headline so far has been something you could use <u>immediately</u> to make money, either

a)   without changing it (if it's for your business) or

b)   with only minor modifications (if it's written for a business close to yours, or if it's a template in Bonus #1).

Now I'd like to tell you about how you can increase the value of your mind just by picking out headlines in your day-to-day doings.

It's really simple. Be like a detective. Be on the lookout for headlines.

This will help you in ways you can't yet even imagine… you'll suddenly become much more attuned to the words of everyday language that are so powerful in selling situations. It will help you not only in writing copy but in persuasive speaking of all sorts.

A few minutes ago I was at Mel's, a San Francisco 50's-style diner. I glanced at the oldies jukebox and realized how many song titles would make good headlines. Check these out: **Let's Get It On**, by Marvin Gaye; **Memories Are Made of This**, Dean Martin; **Stop In the Name of Love**,

The Supremes; **Hello Heartache, Goodbye Love**, Peggy March; and **Shop Around**, The Miracles.

Three of them would probably only work if you were selling something romantically related — but **Memories Are Made of This** and **Shop Around** could work in a lot of situations.

Now, I am <u>not</u> suggesting you use these phrases as headlines in your ads. (You <u>can</u> use any of the 297 variations in the first 20 chapters; they're brand new, just for you. But don't use any of the original proven headlines word-for-word.) In fact, my advice is <u>never</u> to use a headline or title from another ad word-for-word as the headline for your ad. And that goes especially for song titles, since the Recording Industry Association of America is pretty possessive of its intellectual property, as the Napster court battles demonstrated.

So here's what I <u>am</u> suggesting: Keep your radar on at all times for good phrases that could be <u>adapted</u> for new headlines.

For example, today I was reading the highbrow *Economist* magazine and ran across this wonderful headline: **How to make deeply suspicious people want to give you lots and lots of money**. It was for a book on writing business plans to raise venture capital.

Then I was reading another one of my favorite weekly publications, the lowbrow *National Enquirer*. I saw a headline that stopped me in my tracks: **Are you KILLING yourself and the ones you love?** It was for a new product that reduces "harmful electromagnetic waves emitted during cellular and cordless phone use."

Here's another one from the *Enquirer*: **Spider Veins Gone Guaranteed!** It's for Veinish — no, I'm not making this up — which you rub on your legs and it makes spider veins disappear.

I have a friend who has a very colorful life story. He's a genius. He's a high school dropout, too. My friend has been a midway barker and pitchman at County Fairs; he's written radio commercials for nationally known celebrities; and sometimes he works as a telemarketer.

I love to talk with this guy. He speaks in headlines and he doesn't even know it. It's in his bones. He's also a very interesting guy, and that's why I love to talk with him. I listen for the headlines, because that keeps my radar finely tuned and keeps me sharp for whenever I have copy to write.

I listen to radio commercials for great phrases and sentences. I remember dialogue from movies that has a special "ring" to it. I do this because it increases and enhances my headline awareness and my headline consciousness. Now, let me make this suggestion: You do the same. It will pay off handsomely, for you, as it has — and does — for me.

To subscribe to David Garfinkel's Copywriting Podcast (it's free), go to:

www.GarfinkelCoaching.com/podcast

PART
II

The Magical Power of Headlines

PART

II

CHAPTER 1

THE IMPORTANCE OF A POWERFUL HEADLINE

To help you understand just why headlines are so important — important enough for me to write a whole book about them — I'd like you to take a quick trip to the streets of Chicago.

In fact, I'd like to invite you to go backwards in time with me. A couple of decades ago, when I lived in the Windy City. At the time, my home was seven blocks away from "Big John," the 100-story John Hancock building.

Now let's say you and I had a meeting scheduled for 10 a.m. Tuesday morning at an office on the 27th floor.

A taxi drops you off in front of 875 N. Michigan Ave. (the address of the John Hancock building). After you get through security, you enter the lobby and head towards the elevators. Get in; push "27"; take a high-speed ride up into the sky; get out; turn right; and you find your way to the office where we're having our meeting.

Simple enough, right?

Well, doing business in real life is very much like the imaginary voyage and meeting you just envisioned.

I'll show you here how it applies to doing business on the Internet:

- *The taxi ride* is like the form of traffic that got you to my Web site.

- *The John Hancock building* is like my Web site itself.

- *The elevator ride* is like reading my Web site, and...

- *Coming into the office on the 27th floor* is like taking the action I wanted you to take — making a purchase; signing up for a newsletter; requesting more information; etc.

But wait a minute! Did you notice I left out a very important part of the process?

Darn right I did. I left out:

- *The front door of the John Hancock building!*

Why is that so important? Because if I can't get you in the front door, then what chance do I have of getting you to the elevator; in the elevator; up 27 floors; and into the office?

Answer: I have no chance at all... until I get you in the front door!

Now, why the convoluted analogy?

Here's why. I've given you this elaborate example to emphasize how *crucial* your headline is to your Web site... or any other piece of sales copy you write (on the Web or off). And yes, you guessed it:

- *The front door of the John Hancock building* is your headline!

And an important front door it is. Advertising experts estimate that between 75% and 90% of any advertising's effectiveness comes from the headline.

Here, then, is why what you learn from this chapter is so vitally important to your success as a marketer:

■   ■   ■

With a good headline, you stand a fighting chance of having anything from minimal to overwhelming success.

But without a good headline, your chances of success are next to zero.

So let's start at the beginning. By the time we're done with this chapter, you will have a whole mini-seminar on headlines under your belt — from the very basic to the moderately advanced. For now, though, we start with the basics:

WHAT IS A HEADLINE?

A headline is the first set of words that your prospect sees on any piece of copy you write. It's just like the headlines you see in a newspaper:

- **Economy Improves As Unemployment Drops, Consumer Spending Swells**

- **Ninth-Inning Grand Slam Saves The Day**

- **Flu Vaccine Shortage Worries Health Officials**

- **Spring Rains Flood Farmlands**

- **New Computer Chip Promises Better Video On Handheld Computers**

While all these headlines would work well to sell newspapers and get readers interested in reading the news stories that follow, only last one would work in marketing, 99% of the time. Why? Because most newspaper-style headlines merely sell the reader on reading the story, but they aren't designed to create interest in, and desire for, a product or service that you'd be telling the prospect about.

However, the last headline in the list — **New Computer Chip Promises Better Video On Handheld Computers** — has a characteristic that could make it work just as well for an ad as for a news story. It's this: The headline conveys a *benefit* ("Better Video on Handheld Computers") of a *product* ("New Computer Chip"), and this not only creates *interest* in the product. It also creates a *desire* for that product — if, that is, you're the kind of person who likes video on your computers.

In short, a headline not only needs to capture attention and keep your prospect reading. It also needs to *set the tone* for what the prospect is about to read — and, to *create a mood* in the prospect that will begin to make him or her receptive to taking the *action* you will eventually invite him or her to take in your sales copy.

That action might be *to buy what you are selling*. It could be just *to request more information*. Or, it might be *to request an application form*, which would lead to the next step of the sales process.

Whatever action it is you desire your prospect to take, your headline has an important job to do: *prepare the prospect emotionally for the invitation you are soon about to make.*

CHAPTER 2

TYPES OF ADVERTISING HEADLINES THAT WORK ON THE WEB

You'll almost always use a *single headline* with the following types of marketing copy:

1. **Sales emails**. When you are sending out an email that requests some sort of action, the subject line of the email serves as your headline.

2. **Short text ads for ezines**. These are short ads, four to 10 lines or so, that publishers run in their email newsletters (ezines). These ads look a lot like classified ads in a newspaper, although sometimes they are considerably longer than the 2-3 lines you see in the paper.

3. **Google AdWords ads**. You've seen these when you use Google, but you might not know what they're called. AdWords ads are the "sponsored listings" in the right-hand column of each page of search engine results. You can buy these (as opposed to search engine listings on the left-hand side, which you have to compete for), and you can even pay for position. If you want to be first ad everyone sees at the top of the heap, it's entirely possible, although in some categories the very top spot might cost more than you want to spend.

But you may *use more than one headline* on...

4. **Web pages**. On a Web site, you may have *multiple headlines* at the top of your page. You might want to use a *pre-head*, which is a short phrase in small type before the headline; a *main headline*, which states the main promise of what you're offering your prospect throughout the copy; and even a *sub-heads* right after the main headline, to flesh out and highlight the benefit that you introduce in your main headline.

We'll cover examples of all types of headlines as we proceed.

CHAPTER 3

WHERE MOST PEOPLE GO WRONG WITH HEADLINES

Headlines can make a tremendous difference in the dollars-and-cents effectiveness of any piece of copy. Changes in a headline can easily double and triple closing rates. I know one marketer who claims *he increased his sales on the same ad 18 times* just by changing the headline!

Most people, unfortunately, write really bad headlines. It's not necessarily that they use bad grammar or spelling. The problem is that their headlines don't "reach people where they live." These headlines don't create interest, desire, and receptivity to taking action. They don't do their job, so they're not good headlines.

Here are the three main underlying causes of headline problems:

1. **The Headline Doesn't Pass The "So What? Who Cares?" Test**. A merely factual headline doesn't cut the mustard, because facts by themselves rarely stir people's emotions. Also, when there's a promise spelled out that the prospect doesn't instantly see as valuable, then the headline doesn't have relevant emotional power — and it, too, fails the test.

2. **The Headline Is Cute, Clever or Obscure**. You see lots of headlines like this. They include plays on words, sexual innuendo, attempts at humor, or displays of what the headline writer thought was exquisite sophistication. While this approach may raise a chuckle and even get the prospect reading the rest of your Web page, unless what's being sold in the copy is *directly* related to the cuteness up top, a headline of this type *never* sets the tone and puts the prospect in the mood most conducive for taking action afterwards.

3. **The Headline Means Everything To The Business But Nothing To The Prospect**. If your company has just celebrated its 25th anniversary, that's terrific! Very few businesses last that long. But a self-congratulatory headline trumpeting that fact has no power to motivate prospects to take action... unless the prospect has a gnawing, burning need to do business with a 25-year-old company, and is *already* aware of that need *before* he or she reads the headline.

Most headline problems can be traced to the failure of person who wrote the headline to stand in the prospect's shoes (mentally), and see things (in his or her mind's eye) from the prospect's point of view. It's a very valuable skill to learn. And it's key to writing good, powerful headlines.

CHAPTER 4

HOW DO YOU KNOW WHAT KIND OF HEADLINE TO WRITE?

Here are five rules of thumb to help you get in the right frame of mind to write a winning headline:

1. **Start where your reader is**. Most people writing copy start where *they* are. This is a big mistake, unless you are selling to peers — people who are as knowledgeable about what you are selling as you are (which is rarely the case). Typically, *starting where your reader* is means, focusing on the biggest *benefit* your product or service provides.

    On the other hand, starting where you are — which, again, you *don't* want to do — means focusing on a *fact, accomplishment or feature* that you consider important, but which will have little or no meaning to your reader.

    Example: You sell office supplies over the Internet. Because of skillfully negotiated contracts with manufacturers, you have wider access to more varieties of products, at lower prices, with faster delivery, than anyone else in your industry.

    Here's a typical example of starting where *you* are:

Our Supply Chain Relationships Are Second To None!

Anyone who wants a stapler or some new inkjet cartridges will have no idea what you're talking about, and couldn't care less about learning more.

Compare that with a headline that starts where the reader is:

Office Supplies: Lowest Prices, Best Selection and Fastest Delivery. We Can Prove It And We Guarantee It!

The second headline is about the benefits of all those skillfully negotiated supply-chain relationships. And anyone looking for office supplies will be motivated to read further.

2. **Look at the end result your reader wants**. As a marketer — whether you're writing copy for your own business, or for someone else's — you have to learn every little detail about products, services and whatever else is for sale. It's easy to get wrapped up in the details and forget that people aren't buying what you're selling — they're really buying *what it can do for them.*

   The O.M. Scott and Sons Company was founded in 1907 as a mail-order seller of grass seed. Mr. Scott once told his employees that their customers weren't buying grass seed from the company; "They're buying greener lawns."

   Your headline is strong and attractive when it talks about the beneficial end result of using what you sell — What is *your* "greener lawn?"

3. **Spell out how what you're selling provides the solution to a problem, or the attainment of a desire**. Once you know where your readers are and what end result they're looking for, figure out

what's on their mind that would lead them to wanting what you have. Chances are very good it's either something that's bothering them, or something they have a strong, persistent desire for, but they haven't been able to get yet.

A golf pro may teach concentration, posture, better swing and better attitude. But what's bothering the golfer is: too many strokes to get to each hole. What the golfer wants is to get to each hole with fewer strokes. A headline that promises fewer strokes and a better score will far outperform a headline that talks about concentration, posture, better swing or better attitude.

4. **Determine how aware your prospects are of their problem and/or desire**. This can be tricky. You've spent a lot of time thinking about what's on your prospects' minds, so you're very aware of how you can solve their problems and help them get what they want. But the same may not be true of your prospects.

Two steps will help you zero-in on this important factor. The first is to talk to people in your target market, and find out what's on their mind. The second step is to figure out how the *consequences* or *implications* of this problem are showing up in their lives.

Suppose you offer a travel package to a little-known South Seas island that provides an unusually wonderful and gratifying relief for stress. All you have to do is go there, and your stress magically disappears. Better than anywhere else in the world.

Your market wants to be relieved of its stress, but people in it may be so stressed out they don't even realize stress is the problem. A little investigation, however, determines that they are quite sure the cause

111

of all their problems is a) their boss, b) the other drivers during their commute, and c) the 437 elected politicians in Washington.

A not-so-good headline for this group would be:

The Perfect Antidote To The Stress That Impairs You

A much better headline for this group would be:

How To Undo What Your Boss... The Rush-Hour Traffic... And Politicians In Washington Are Doing To You

Now, as an expert on stress, you know that Senators, Senior Vice Presidents and SUVs are not the *real* cause of stress in this prospect's life. Fine. But if those are the things on your *market's* mind that can lead them to purchasing your product, then get past what "you know" and get into what "they know." Start there. (And your headline is where you start.)

5. **Bear in mind how many of your competitors your prospect is aware of.** This means that you have to know, first, who your competitors are, and secondly, how much most of your prospects know about them. That requires research.

The more people in your market know about other competitors, the more work you have to do in differentiating what you have to offer as to how it provides greater value. A lower price is one way. Superior performance and other unique benefits is usually a better way. Highlight your best differentiating benefit in your headline.

CHAPTER 5

WHAT DO WINNING HEADLINES LOOK LIKE?

L et's start with classic headlines, and then we'll look at specific applications of headline-writing for the Internet.

Here are a half a dozen time-tested headlines. (What you're about to see is a short set of examples for how you can use the templates in Part I of this book.)

Note: These headlines, modified for a particular product or service, still work like crazy today! I'll give you an example after each one:

1. **The Secret Of Making People Like You**
   Example of Modification:
   The Secret Of Sleeping Well Without Drugs

2. **Are You Ever Tongue-Tied At A Party?**
   Example of Modification:
   Do You Ever "Trip Over Your Own Tongue" During A Sales Presentation?

3. **How To Win Friends And Influence People**
   Example of Modification:
   How To Create A Website And Make Money While You Sleep

Incidentally, you may think of original headline #3 as a book title. It is. But it was also a headline of a very successful ad used to sell the book!

4. **Who Else Wants A Screen Star Figure?**
   Example of Modification:
   Who Else Wants 'Killer Abs' With No Hard Work?

5. **Discover The Fortune That Lies Hidden In Your Salary**
   Example of Modification:
   Discover The Fortune That Lies Hidden In Your Basement And Attic

6. **Here's A Quick Way To Break Up A Cold**
   Example of Modification:
   Here's A Quick Way To Get Your Website Up And Running

I've given you these examples so you will have a point of reference for what makes an indisputably good headline. Here are some key points to notice about all of them:

■ Each headline points to an *end result*, and that is what people are looking for most of the time. Some of the end results in the original headlines: "People Like You"; "(*implied benefit*: **not** being) Tongue-Tied At A Party"; "Win Friends And Influence People"

■ The headlines are made from *short words*. Most are one-syllable words, and in all six original headlines, there's only one three-syllable word: influence.

■ These headlines both arouse curiosity and stoke desire. The copywriters probably thought long and hard about what people *really* want before they settled on the final version of the headline, and, they artfully arranged the words to make people reading them wonder "what's this about?" as they felt an inner emotional tug moving them towards getting the end result.

CHAPTER 6

REAL WORLD EXAMPLES: HEADLINES FROM INTERNET MARKETING

N ow that you understand the psychology and function of headlines, and you've seen some examples of winning headlines from the real world of paid advertising, you're in a much better position to take advantage of what you're about to learn.

So let's get into the nitty-gritty. It was important to lay the groundwork first, because effective headlines are almost like a foreign language to most people, even though the words are all in English!

EMAIL SUBJECT LINES

An important principle to burn into your brain is, *it's very, very risky (and difficult) to* **start** *an Internet relationship with a prospect using email.* That's because of the spam problem. Email is inherently a very personal medium, so you're better off getting prospects through search engines, ads in ezines, pay-per-click ads (like Google AdWords) and referrals from other Web sites and email lists where people already have a relationship with another person or business.

Email is most effective, then, when you *already* have a relationship of some sort with a prospect or customer.

Bear that in mind as you look at these examples:

Dr. Dave Woynarowski is a physician who has come up with pharmaceutical-grade supplements that also use alternative-healing ingredients. He has a daily email newsletter that talks about his supplements in relation to various health issues. Here are some excellent subject lines he has used:

- **How to Energize Your Life!**

- **Fish Oil and Lung Cancer**

- **Sacred Cow, or a Pile of Cow Dung?**

Just as with any kind of headline, the key to writing successful subject lines is knowing what's of interest to your reader, and starting where your reader is. Dr. Dave has the advantage of a full patient load at his medical clinic, so he knows first-hand what's on the mind of his customers. You don't need to be a doctor, though, to engage in some kind of dialogue with your customers and prospects — and it's important that you do.

Now, to someone who's never heard of Dr. Dave and isn't familiar with his supplements and his philosophy, these subject lines could come across somewhere between meaningless and annoying. But to his loyal and informed readership, these are excellent phrases... they cause interest and prompt the reader to open the email and read it.

I know that for a fact. How come? Because I'm one of his customers, and I'm interested in what he has to say.

Incidentally, if you're curious, you can find out more about what Dr. Dave's up to at **www.DrDavesBest.com.**

■   ■   ■

HEADLINES FOR SMALL ADS ON THE INTERNET

Small classified ads are different from emails, in that they will not be seen as intrusive if you don't already have a relationship with the person reading them. You typically pay to place these ads in ezines, or on Web sites.

Headlines are like the headlines on Google AdWords ads, and single headlines for Web pages — both covered below — so we won't spend a lot of time with small ads.

Here are a couple to look at:

Become a Best-Selling Author Online!
Ebooks are a low-cost, high-profit way
to make money on the Internet, and you
can become an author even if you don't
write the ebook yourself! Learn how.
http://www.EbookSecretsExposed.com

How to Meet a '10' on the Internet
It all starts with your picture. No matter
what you look like, the odds are high
that your online photo isn't doing
you justice. Get a top pro trained to
take pictures that look GREAT for
Internet dating, at a reasonable price!
http://www.DateBetter.com

Notice the headlines (in boldface type) follow the same rules that we've been talking about all along: they feature a beneficial end result, they are designed to stoke desire, they use short words, and they put the reader in the frame of mind to read more and possibly to take action.

GOOGLE ADWORDS ADS

Google AdWords ads are in a special category all by themselves. They're small ads that appear on the right hand side of the results page when you do a search on Google.

Here's one that I wrote:

> **Hot New MLM**
> This one puts money in your pocket
> two ways. Get your share! Aff.
> www.DavidGarfinkel.com/travel

What's the headline? "Hot New MLM." My 12th-grade English teacher at Richard Montgomery High School in Rockville, Maryland, would have flunked me for writing a sentence like that. But the marketplace — that is, the people who typed "MLM" into Google — gave me an "A."

I got 3.5% of the people who saw a page where this ad appeared, to click on it. (Google requires a minimum of 0.5% click-throughs to keep an ad running. My ad performed at *seven times the minimum*. Not a world record — not even a personal best for me — but very successful, nonetheless.)

A couple points about this headline:

- *Relevancy*. People who saw this ad had "MLM" on the brain — because those are the letters they had typed into Google in the first place. So I'm already a step ahead because I'm talking about what they're already looking for.

- *Emotion*. The other two words in the headline, "Hot" and "New," spark excitement. For a contrasting example to put this in perspective, imagine if I had used "Old, Cold MLM" as my headline! (Yes, it would have worked *great* as a *joke*, but in the serious, grown-up world of actually getting results and making money, it would have flopped like a gasping fish on a dry dock.)

Here's another very successful AdWords ad:

Beat the AdWords System
Access 100 Million People in 10 Min
The Definitive Fast Start Guide
http://Copy.AdwordsAdvertising.com

This is an ad that pops up when people type "Google AdWords" into Google. It's the work of Perry Marshall, who, for my money, is the preeminent authority on using this advertising medium to get results.

Perry's headline is clever, in a productive way. "Beat the AdWords System" implies there is a system, which, of course most people don't know about; that it's possible to beat the system (which is inherently appealing, all by itself); and that he can show you how.

And, once again, there's a word in the headline ("AdWords") that was already on the propsect's mind (because that's what he or she typed into the search form in order for the ad to come up). That's very important.

Copywriting legend Robert Collier, who sold millions of books in the 1930s through direct mail and advertising, admonishes copywriters to "enter the conversation already going on in the prospect's mind."

By using the same words they typed into the search engine in your ad, you're pretty much guaranteed to do that.

Now, check out this AdWords ad:

Free Ebook on Recording
The tools and support to make audio
information products on your PC.
http://www.RecordYourself.com

It's for a very specialized market: people who publish ebooks on the Internet, and want to make audio recordings of their ebooks so their customers will have another way to purchase, and take in, the information.

Mike Stewart, who goes by the moniker "The Internet Audio Guy," wrote this ad. It shows up when people type things like "record yourself" and "recorded ebook" into Google.

The headline is great, because it makes a *free offer*. Anytime you can give something away for free that your market will perceive as valuable (and related to what they're looking for that you can provide them) — do it.

Notice again that neither the headline nor the rest of the ad adheres to the rules of English composition. No matter. Mike says he gets plenty of business from this little ad, and as you study it, you can see why.

HEADLINES FOR WEB SITES

The same rules apply for Web site headlines, but with a twist... you can have more than one headline. This is especially the case when your Web site is selling something that has a lot of desirable dimensions to it and you want to get your prospect mentally prepared to learn about a lot of different benefits.

Here's what I call a "headline package" for a very successful site selling a self-improvement course:

Wanted: People Who
Need Money FAST!

How YOU can *cash in* on the
$25,000-a-day secret that's *made millions*

The first headline is actually a banner graphic that runs across the top of Web site. "How to Get Lots of Money for Anything — Fast!" is the title of the book, but, it's also a very compelling headline.

"Wanted: People Who Need Money FAST!" is the second headline. To the *rational* mind, this is obviously redundant. But to the *emotional* mind, this is very telling. It says, "Oh! They're looking for people like me" — if, that is, the prospect is someone who needs money fast.

The third headline, "How YOU can cash in on the $25,000-a-day secret that's made millions," again, seems to be repeating what the first two headlines are saying. But take a closer look. The third headline takes a big, conceptual promise and makes it a little more specific. Now the reader's curiosity and desire are building to a fever pitch.

And that's exactly what a headline — or, in this case, a headline package — is supposed to do. For more information about this course, visit http://www.GetAnythingFast.com.

Now, here's a headline for an audio CD / searchable ebook package about dream interpretation:

123

WARNING:

Your Dreams Are
"911 Emergency Calls"
From Your Subconscious Mind!

Don't Ignore Them. They're Trying to Tell You Something.

There are three parts to this Web page headline:

1. "WARNING": The pre-head

2. "Your Dreams Are '911 Emergency Calls" From Your Subconscious Mind!" — the main headline

3. "Don't Ignore Them, They're Trying to Tell You Something" — the sub-head.

People who come to this Web site have clicked on links in ads or articles that talk about the interpretation of dreams. It's a pre-selected group of prospects — the perfect target market for this product.

This headline package is what I refer to as a "wake-up call" (pun intended). Though some people wake up in a cold sweat, and trembling, from a particularly horrible nightmare, most people are at most confused by their dreams, or else ignore them altogether, and in any event, don't give them a second thought.

The owner of this Web site, Dr. Michael Wolf, is a clinical psychologist who knows better. He realizes that dreams have great importance, although most people will do anything not to get the message. That is why he chose to inject so much shock-value into the headline package.

As you can see, besides sounding an alarm, this headline package arouses great curiosity in the reader and makes him or her highly receptive to the solution that will be offered later on the Web page.

You can see the whole Web page at: **http://www.Dream-Analyst.com**.

Another example:

Adriana Dodge is a real estate expert who has put together a manual, which includes legal documents, for people who want to buy a home but wouldn't qualify financially under normal conditions. Here is the headline package for her Web site:

Get our FREE newsletter about how you can buy a home with No cash and even No credit. Sign up now!

The header graphic contains the first headline: "Adriana Dodge's No Cash No Credit Home Buying System." Her name starts the headline because the way she drives traffic to the site is by radio interviews. People already know her name, and may even feel like they know her a little bit.

The last seven words of this top headline tell the whole story about her product while extolling its benefits. The benefits more or less describe the target market — people who have little cash and possibly bad credit, who want to buy a house.

The second headline, "Get our FREE newsletter about how you can buy a home with No Cash and even No Credit. Sign up now!", makes a very appealing offer that, once accepted, begins a non-threatening relationship between Adriana and the prospect.

Adriana's free newsletter gives her a way to begin communication with wary prospects; build trust; and eventually make more sales than if she depended solely on the one visit to the site to get her all her business.

More information at: **http://www.AskAdriana.com**.

And finally, here's the headline package I wrote for the first issue of my own "World Copywriting Newsletter":

The Tip of the Iceberg
Or, How An Advertising Secret That Created A Six-Year Backlog In Order For Pianos Can Get You More Business Than You Ever Imagined Was Possible!

The main headline, "The Tip of the Iceberg," could mean just about anything, but it has a dual emotional appeal: first, it could mean "danger ahead"; second, it could refer to a visible clue of a much larger and more substantial something-or-other beneath the surface.

The second headline, "Or, How An Advertising Secret That Created A Six-Year Backlog In Orders for Pianos Can Get You More Business Than You Ever Imagined Was Possible!", creates closure for the ambiguity caused by the first headline, but opens up even more ambiguity to keep the reader reading!

126

It creates closure by making more tangible what "The Tip of the Iceberg" means. Clearly, it means something about an advertising secret.

But when you learn that this secret created a six-year backlog in orders ... and that this secret can work for your business as well... this creates a wracking curiosity that can only be relieved by continuing to pay attention and read the newsletter.

By the way, if you'd like to see my newsleter yourself, it's free to subscribe. Go to: **http://www.World-Copywriting-Institute.com**.

CHAPTER 7

10 GOLDEN RULES FOR WRITING POWERFUL HEADLINES

We've covered a lot so far, and if you mind is awhir from all the information and examples, I don't blame you one bit.

It took me about 30 years of working on newspapers, magazines and my own books (on the content-producing, editorial side) along with 15 years of writing copy and teaching others to do the same (many of those were the same years... I'm not that old!) to learn what I've just shared with you.

I've found that simple rules of thumb are very helpful in assimilating new knowledge and translating it into productive action. With that in mind, here are five "do's" and five "don'ts" to guide your headline writing, both on the Internet and in non-Internet (print, radio and tv) formats.

DO'S:

1. **Make it conversational.** Learn how people talk, and even how you talk when you're not being self-conscious or trying to sound "professional." Strive to put that in your copywriting — *especially*

your headlines. The more it sounds like real conversation, the more engaging it will be for your reader.

2.   **Enter the conversation already going on in the customer's mind**. This famous piece of advice from 1930's copywriting legend Robert Collier may be the single most important thing to remember when you start writing copy. It's a more specific version of my rule: Start where the *reader* is, not where you are.

3.   **Remember "V.E.R.V.E"** — **Visceral, Emotional, Resounding, Visual, Empathic**. It's a memory-jogger to help you build the kind of headlines that get results. Point-by-point:

   ■   **Visceral** literally means having to do with your intestines — your guts. A visceral headline is very physical and immediate.

   ■   **Emotional** means, the headline appeals to your reader's *feelings*.

   ■   **Resounding** means it sounds like someone talking. Your reader can "hear" you saying the headline, because it comes across as conversational language.

   ■   **Visual** means the reader can *picture* what your headline is about

   ■   **Empathic** means the reader feels you understand how he or she feels

4.   **Walk the fine line between fact and hype**. A timid headline won't do you any good, but neither will one that is so over-the-top that no one will believe it. Make the biggest claim you can make, and still prove in your copy.

5.   **Understand the ultimate purpose of your headline is to get your reader to read the next line of copy**. Don't sum up everything you're

about to say later in your headline. Create intrigue, curiosity and desire. Leave 'em hungry for more!

DON'TS:

1. **Don't be clever.** Most of the time, the urge to be clever is a short-cut to avoid doing the work of creating an enticing promise that will prepare the reader to take the action you are looking for. Resist the temptation; a straightforward headline almost always works better than a clever one.

2. **Don't be boring.** Remember that ultimately, what you are looking for is *action*. Action involves *motion*. Motion is prompted by *emotion*. And emotion is generated by *excitement*. Don't settle for a headline that is more likely to produce a yawn than anything else.

3. **Don't assume your prospect knows what you know.** It's easy to fall into the trap of forgetting all the time and effort you put into building the knowledge and expertise you have on the product, service or information you are marketing. Make the effort to turn back the clock, in your mind, to when you knew far less. Don't write your headline for sophisticated people; write for the person who needs to learn more.

4. **Don't focus on your process.** Remember Mr. Scott and the grass seed? People aren't interested, initially, in how the seeds are selected, or developed, or, for that matter, stored or shipped. People are interested in greener lawns, their end result. Don't focus on your process; focus on what the prospect *gets*.

5. **Don't merely try to arouse curiosity**. You have to do better than that if you want your prospect to get up enough of an emotional head of steam to be ready to buy, or take some other crucial action, after they finish reading your copy. Curiosity at the outset won't do it. Curiosity's good, but what's more important is desire. And intrigue.

CONCLUSION

YOUR NEXT STEP

By now you can see the power of these Advertising Headlines. They have taken a difficult and uncertain task, and changed it to an easy one where you have certainty about your headline... and even a good idea about where to go next as you put your winning advertising copy together!

But there's more. Author David Garfinkel has created an entire, comprehensive and easy-to-use System for writing advertising. His System is called *Copywriting Templates*. It makes every step of the process as easy as it is now for you to write headlines.

Take your advertising power to the next level. Go to:

HTTP://WWW.WORLD-COPYWRITING-INSTITUTE.COM/AH-TEMPLATES

Printed in the USA
CPSIA information can be obtained
at www.ICGtesting.com
JSHW082352140824
68134JS00020B/2029

9 781683 501459